Ain't No Change!

Muaty Poets

LEGACY

Compilation Volume 2, Album Companion Book

For information contact: info@uptownmediaventures.com

Book and Cover design by Team Uptown

ISBN: 978-1-68121-044-5

First Edition: December 2016

10 9 8 7 6 5 4 3 2 1

Dedicated to Russell Atkins and Norman Jordan who were instrumental in the formation of the Muntu Poets.

To all the socially conscious literary minded poets, writers, musicians, painters, and all-around "cool cats."

Muntu

Derived from African Zulu culture that means a human being, sometimes used to mean "a Black person."

THE
MUNTU POETS
OF CLEVELAND

the
Muntu
poets

Table of Contents

Foreword

Like the tone and tenor when The Muntu Poets first arrived on the cultural and political scene of the turbulent mid '60s to the early '70s in the City of Cleveland, they have re-grouped over forty years later and are as relevant and provocative as ever. Their arrival on that scene was described in the introduction of *Muntu Poets Anthology Volume 2: 47 Years Later with Russell Atkins* - "They reflected the rage, dissent, and rebellious nature of the community during this time. The group consisted of several young members from every political stripe, from liberal to radical."

The group formed out of the leadership and tutelage of two exceptionally accomplished writer/poets: Russell Atkins and Norman Jordan. Russell Atkins, a major composer-editor-poet, used revolutionary musical structures in his writing, co-founding possibly the oldest black literary magazine in the country, *Freelance*, in 1950. Norman Jordan went on to become one of the most noted writers of the Black Arts Movement and have his work published in over 40 publications and plays performed internationally.

Four of the Muntu poets were in the movie *Uptight,* directed by Jules Dassin. Russell Atkins, Amir Rashidd, Yahya Abdussabur, and C.E. Shy. The movie was produced in 1968 in Cleveland, Ohio. Shortly after the film was released, the Glenville riots broke out.

The Muntu Poets' Volume 2 Anthology was a dedication to Russell Atkins and Norman Jordan and spearheaded by one of the original members of The Muntu Poets, C.E. Shy. Who knew that this would be the result of C.E. Shy contacting most of the original Muntu Poets and putting the proverbial "band and back together again," so to speak. Now we have the first Compilation CD Albums along with Companion Books for each volume. The Albums and the respective Companion Books of Collected Poems is named - what else - *Straight Up!* and *Ain't No Change!,* respectively.

There are reasons why I will cherish these Compilations and Companion Books. First off, the artistic effort that has come to fruition has its own value in the historical context of when and why The Muntu Poets came to exist. It was during a cataclysmic period in this country's Civil Rights struggle and the Black Arts Movement; and its re-discovery and intense identification with African History that deeply impacted the political awareness of the urban grassroots. Secondly, I get to savor the multifaceted beauty of both albums: These are poets who have matured yet definitely have NOT forgotten from whence they have come. These cats are now grandfathers, pillars of the community, one of them is even an active Imam.

The themes and moods range from angrily militant and political to heartbreakingly tender and romantic, to spiritual and fly old school *"lean & pull-a-chick"* *lyricisms.* The musical accompaniment ranges from Jazz, The Blues, Hip Hop, Classical and R&B.

Finally, these albums and their companion books are indeed trailblazers and will become more precious as the years progress. These "artifacts" are a witness to what a consciously evolved black man looks like having come of age during a period of riots, crime, poverty and, last but not least, a steadfast adherence to his muscular spirituality and artistic visions. I must say that these albums even one up the seminal 1970 album *The Last Poets*.

Completely accessible to both older and younger audiences, with a new millennium feel, that is trail blazing new artistic territory. Words cannot do these two classics justice which, to date, are unparalleled.

You will thoroughly enjoy these joints – *Straight Up!*

Winston Gragg
President
African American Music Association
Cleveland, Ohio

THE MUNTU POETS
ANTHOLOGY VOLUME 2
47 Years Later
WITH RUSSELL ATKINS

Introduction

The genesis of The Muntu Poets Legacy and Uptown Records occurred in a very unusual fashion. The Muntu Poets were in the process of publishing the anthology *Muntu Poets 47 Years later with Russell Atkins*, during the time frame in question.

To be honest, as the publisher of Uptown MJV Publishing, I was not paying much attention to the written works. I was in earnest attempting to collate all the poems, pictures and writer's bios into the nearly 200 page anthology.

One evening Mr. Gentleman, aka C.E. Shy, read a piece called *The Beast*. He read the passage with great emphasis and flair. I was floored!

"That has to be recorded!" I exclaimed.

That day was the genesis of Uptown MJV Records and, of course, the Muntu Poets Legacy. The process has been fraught with challenges but the end results (nearly 100 recordings of poetry with musical accompaniment) has been greatly rewarding!

Because many of the Muntu Poets are older and are located around the continental United States, some of the recordings were not done live in a studio. The Poets simply made recordings with whatever recording device available at their disposal. Many used their cell phones!

The end results have been surprisingly dramatic!

Also, there is a young clique, of poets, singers and rappers, that is following in the footsteps of the Muntu Poets – the Legacies. They embody the resilient spirit and determination displayed by all the Muntu Poets from the 1960s onward.

The eclectic display of the multifaceted talents of the Muntu Poets is indeed fascinating. Enjoy!

K Kelly McElroy
Cleveland, Ohio

Mr. Gentleman aka C.E. Shy

Biographical Information

Mr. Gentleman aka C.E. Shy, an original Muntu Poet, has been writing since the seventh grade. He continued through high school, until he became more involved in sports. After graduating, he worked at the White Motors Company, where he was involved with the company's newspaper. He started a column called: "the Poets Corner." That was his first published work.

He moved to Sweden after he left the "States" with a one way ticket. He met an English photographer and started writing narratives, for some of the photographs that would be sold to newspapers and magazines.

After returning to the States, he joined a poetry workshop, the Muntu Poets, run by Russell Atkins and Norman Jordan from 1966 to 1968. He stopped writing for years, then started back writing again in late 1990's; when he started writing novellas and flash fiction, in addition to poetry. He joined a poetry workshop in Lyndhurst, Ohio at the county library in 2011 to hone his writing skills. He has been published in two anthologies and in the 60's in the Muntu Poets book of poems done by Russell Atkins and Norman Jordan.

Literary Works

Books

Substitutions
Time Share
Eclections 2
Eclections 3
Powhims and Proz
The House
Stories – The Long and the Short of It
Approaching the Ninth Dimension
Raw Forms, Structures and Vicissitudes
Me and Maysun
Deliver Me From Unconsciousness
The Visit
The Door at the End of the Hall
No U Turns One Way
Point Blank! Eclections 4
The Glimpse – A Remote View

Anthologies

The Muntu Poets of Cleveland Volume 1
Cuyahoga County Library Anthologies Volumes 1 - 4
The Muntu Poets 47 Years Later with Russell Atkins

Publications

White Motors

Substitutions
C.E. Shy
ECLECTIONS 2

Time Share
C.E. Shy
ECLECTIONS 3

WORDS IN THE
WIND
A BOOK OF POETIC PROSE BY
C.E SHY

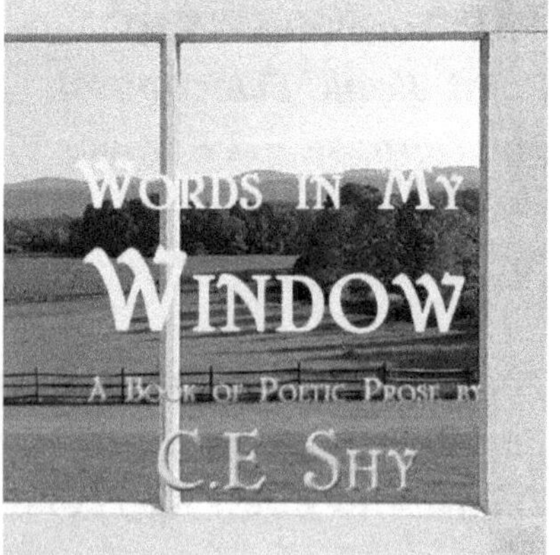
WORDS IN MY
WINDOW
A BOOK OF POETIC PROSE BY
C.E SHY

Fictitious

My right to life---Fictitious

My freedom of movement---Fictitious

Rights as a human---Fictitious

My freedom of speech ...Fictitious

Lust for blood... Delicious

Having no conscience... Permissive

Equal opportunities --- Fictitious

Justice for all of us---Fictitious

Liberty for all of us---Fictitious

Objective opinions for us---Fictitious

Public opinion---Fictitious

Daily news--- Fictitious

Hollywood movies--- Fictitious

Fair play and balance--- Fictitious

Government for all the people---Fictitious

 Milk of human kindness---Fictitious

Nightly news ---Fictitious

Fixing the environment---Fictitious

Loving thy neighbors---Fictitious

Believing in God... Suspicious?

How Come?

The stars seemed so much closer that night.
Their brilliance almost licked me.
Then there was also you. My emotions
leaned on you and expected a reaction.
Our breathing at one time was in sync.
I surrounded you with me.

We were a story whose words had not
come together. There was a theme and a ending
waiting. Your voice was resurrected,
 peeling back the layers that repressed
the memory of it. Part of the past I yearned
returned.

Now, I stand by your grave for an hour or more.
With flowers wilting in my hand as the
minute hand scales the clock's face.
 I stare through thick things cold and
dark and see you on the other side.

It was only
then I knew how Much I loved you.

C. E.
SHY

THE
HOUSE
C.E. SHY

STORIES
THE LONG AND
THE SHORT OF IT
C.E.
SHY
ARMCHAIR
CHRONICLES
ME AND
MAYSUN
C.E. SHY
WITH
MAYSUN SHAHEED

The Chitterling Throne

There they sit, king and queen.
 Keeping the chitterlings clean.
Raising the prince and princess
telling them "it's a culture thing"
on how to respect the chitterling.
How to prepare themselves mentally
to inhale the toilet smells. How
the stuff is full of benefits and a daily
dose of vitamin A. How they must
obey all the rules.

When the debris is cooked and done
 You must hide them in the vegetable
bin just in case some of your folks come in.
Then onhow to
disguise that horrible smell, with air wick
or raid even glade worked well.
Cornbread and coleslaw are the order
of the day it's these two items that keeps the
gout away.

Approaching
The Ninth
Deminsion
C.E.
Shy
Deliver
Me From
Un
conscious
ness
C.E.
Shy

Raw Forms,
Structures and
Vicissitudes of
the
Neighborhood
C.E.
Shy
THE
VISIT
PASSPORT
C.E.
Shy

In Sight

He was considered legally
blind from behind.
His insight was prophetic.
Down the road was his
forte. He was skill -less in
pleasing the crowds. He thought
out loud. He never engaged in
the back and forth of who was right.
He would extinguish the
 excuse before it
could come out from between
decaying teeth and
lopsided tongues. He usually
 looked the same
in daylight. It was nighttime
when he would
change. He was surrounded
by various images
of himself . When others
guessed... He had
insight.

Four of the Muntu poets were in the movie *Uptight,* directed by Jules Dassin: Russell Atkins, Amir Rashidd, Yahya Abdussabur, and C.E. Shy.

The movie was made in Cleveland, Ohio 1968. Shortly after the film was released, the Glenville riots broke out.

Art Nixon

Biographical Information

Art Nixon, living in the Los Feliz Village District of Los Angeles, California, became interested in writing after being introduced to poetry as a member of the Muntu Poets of Cleveland writing workshop headed by Russell Atkins. He wrote and performed his poetry as a member of the Muntu Poets, eventually performing his poetry with various poetry groups locally, at colleges, around the state, and on area radio stations. His interest in writing led him to write essays and poetry for *Black Ascensions* literary and was one of four founders/editors which included Anthony fudge, Larry Howard, and Larry Wade [RIP] in the early 70s. The magazine was a first for Cuyahoga Community College and went on to earn honorable mention for college magazines in *Essence Magazine*.

A Cum Laude Graduate of Case Western Reserve University while married with a 3 year old son, he brought the child to class frequently when babysitters weren't available. [His son is now a professor at a major Los Angeles University with two award winning books and a third just published, "Race On The QT: Blackness in The Films of Quentin Tarantino," University of Texas Press]. Nixon published papers in Academic Journals as an undergraduate, while employed as a module tutor/instructor at Cuyahoga Community College's writing Lab. He also was employed as a visiting Poet-At-Large for the Cleveland Area Arts Council, introducing Greater Cleveland high school, middle school and elementary students to the first celebrated African American poets as early as 18th century slaves Phyllis Wheatley and Juniper Harmon, the Harlem Renaissance writers to those of contemporary urban poetry.

In Los Angeles, Nixon worked as a security guard for many years while writing screenplays, plays, and TV pilots, none of which he was able to get produced. He also wrote a weekly column for now defunct Las Vegas and Los Angeles black focused newspapers, Bronze News and Balance News for several years. He has been published in several poetry anthologies, including *Black American Literature Forum, The Drumming Between Us, Catch The Fire: A Cross-Generational Anthology of African American Poetry,* and others.

He is included in Columbia Granger's Index of African American Poets. Currently, he is working on the novelization of one of his screenplays. It was published as a short story in Robert Fleming's anthology of short stories, *Too Much Boogie: Erotic Remixes of The Dirty Blues*. He has two sons and two grandkids. He is recently retired as front desk manager at The Beverly Hilton Hotel.

Literary Works

<u>Anthologies</u>

Black American Literature Forum
The Drumming Between Us
*Catch The Fire: A Cross-Generational Anthology of
        African American Poetry*
 The Muntu Poets of Cleveland Volume 1
Voices from Leimert Park: a poetry anthology
The Muntu Poets 47 Years Later with Russell Atkins
Too Much Boogie: Erotic Remixes of The Dirty Blues

La Curandera of Montery Road
(for Mary)

You

Magic lady, even before I knew your name

Pushed buttons you had no right to have in your
possession.

You,

Hibiscus-scented sorceress, carried with you

In the secret pockets

Of your black Donna Karan ground length poncho,

The maps to places in my heart I swore never, ever
existed.

You,

With your Rainforest hair of moonless nights

And lips the color of heart-blood

Till this day pierce me with dried Arizona cactus
thorns & thistles where

It hurts...yet feels too good to breathe,

That place where you press the thumb against the heart.

II

In a trance

I have followed you into the desert at night,

Like a child promised endless sweets the color of gemstones.

There,

On the moon-washed desert floor

Your eyes command me to s

To watch you disrobe & move

Naked

And wild

And raunchy to sounds that only you can hear:

the stomping of sharp-booted heels

on hard flamenco wood,

stomping faster & faster in a

Mad staccato clapping and racing fingers

Over guitar strings greased with fresh habanero,

Faster and faster that only your head can hear.

Your body,

The texture of damp moss at dawn—spinning

Your body

Musking the place between sand & diamond-blasted
night sky

With the heavy ripe of fresh slit cantaloupe and salty
Gamay—Twirling &

Gyrating & undulating—shaking stars loose with your
hips and fingertips,

Squatting & Arching

—Lo *quiero ahora!!*

Stomping & pumping

—Lo quiero ahora!

Pumping and pitching

—Te quiero follar!!!!

Pulsing & promising

Gone...**&**...

...Vanished...

In my head

Your voice echoes your home-grown

Riddle of senseless charm but deadly spell—

The only incantation you know:

>	*Lust is love and love is lust,*

>	*Make one your hearts desire*

>	*But never ever trust trust*

i sit bewitched,

touched crazy mad in a moon-soaked desert,

The breeze disguised as your breath on my neck,

Your laughing wrapped in wind…

III

In my bed. Alone.

I rationalize you into something I can handle: Like

Burning up bad karma.

Mid-life confusion.

An inconvenient period of
insanity.

Or just plain old poor judgment.

But inside it is my heart

That knows I am lying.

It giggles secretly to itself,

Knowing it has been healed,

And it knows what I may never admit:

That your spirit is pure heat,

pure ice blue flame for

sterilizing and cauterizing,

old dreams, old

wounds...

and the evidence

of charred moth wings

will always

betray

your presence

in the silence

of my

nights.

Art Nixon 1997

Art Nixon is a contributing writer in *Catch the Fire!!! A Cross-Generational Anthology of Contemporary African-American Poetry*

Art Nixon is a contributing writer in the *Voices from
Leimert Park: a poetry anthology*

Falling & Flying
(for Deena)

Here's a little ditty
'Bout a girl i done fell for named Deena,
You'd fall for too if you seen her

Let me tell you:

i got a fetish for her eyes
But i'm always sneak'n glances at her thighs
& daydreaming 'bout her butt,
'cause i'm too shy to tell her what's "really up."

See, i'm telling you:

i loves to fantasize 'bout her peachy lips,
Pure sublime to watch her drink exotic teas in sensual
sips,
just loves to hear her laugh,
You'd swear i was tick'n her while taking her bath.

Yeah, i'm talk'n 'bout YOU *Deena Rusch*!!!
[Pssst...the girl can play Beethoven & got a gorgeous
tush]

i jest loves to watch her dance,
My Jewish princes in a trance

Contrapuntal legs & feet & hands /spell-casting between
drum beats,
Sucking oxygen from the air/replacing it with heat
Watch her do her rhythmic fling & flounce,
Spell-locked in her special Jewish/African booty-bounce.

Lawd, i'm so upset. Y'all...please *pray* for me!
And y'all *pray* for her!!
Pray we gone dance together
Do'n it forever /even in the hereafter!!

 --Art Nixon 2011

How We Roll

All the Cabernet is gone.

The wedding invitations are finished.

The rinds of Camembert,

A pinch of Beluga,

Half a baguette and three strawberries

Are what's left in the wicker on the grass...

Face to face

Smile to smile

Love eyes for love eyes,

We lean away from each other,

Both hands pulling against both hands:

    feet turned out

    silly in ecstasy

    we let our blades spin us

    in a fast orbit atop

    the concrete table in the park.

Our faces tilt child-like to the sky

We watch the sun get broad-sided by clouds,

Low &
thick,

Dark, they squat/Merge/ knit themselves into long

Shadow-colored blankets of frown:

    So threatening/ the air chills

    So close/they could be touched

    So mad angry/they burst

The city's parks empty themselves,

Urban perpetrators of every ilk

Go deep cover with everybody else.

Cold rain/ fat drops/ crude and rude

Private picnic crashing gangster weather

On the stealth: black clouds breaking

Wide enough to let *The Devil beat his wife*

Real good: Suddenly, crazy sunshine with cold rain

rinsing out the greasy L.A air /Damp-mops

All movement on the streets & sidewalks into

High sheen corridors of slick space and puddles

   It's just you and me, baby love

Hand and hand we proceed

Without their blessings and the RSVP's

Of family and thought-they-were-our friends.

Helmets and knee pads in place/we race

Holding our arms high, high as we can/we roll

Rolling/ Our finger tips stretch way, way

Over our heads/our salty rain-glazed faces turned
skyward,

Reaching, we snatch clumps of icky cloud-dank

And flings it at each other,

Giggle at the funny sound the rain

Makes in our throats when we laugh.

We blade down hills,

Thru intersections &

Red lights impotent

In the face of our

Joy

Our nerve

Our velocity!

From on high

We strike the most curious image:

holding hands (and our breath) as we

as we blade-spray our way thru quick flesh

bodies of dirty street lakes,

sail curbs, stoop, swoop and glide,

Fly, lean on rushed banisters of wind.

My agility/ Watusi & Loose,

Your instincts/ Latin & rhythmically driven:

Taking on blind corners & sharp curves...

From up above we could easily be mistaken

For some kind of strange & graceful Demons

On a glass surface where hell,

At least for the time being,

Has— Lo and Behold—Frozen over!

-Art Nixon 2010

The Original Muntu Poets workshop located on the 2nd
floor at the intersection of Ansel Road and Superior
Avenue, Cleveland, Ohio.
(Photo credit: Yaseen A. Assami)

Yaseen Assami

Biographical Information

Yaseen Assami , aka Perry Wesley Davis, was born on November 12, 1948 in Knoxville, Tennessee. After high school he moved to Cleveland, Ohio.

Here he met several of his long-time friends and Russell Atkins. He, subsequently, became a part of the Muntu Poets. His stay with the Muntu Poets was of short duration but his involvement was very influential and an important part of his development as a youth and a young expressionist writer. Assami counts Russell Atkins as a very good friend and a mentor; a person of unparalleled talent and creative ability. He counts his association with Russell Atkins as an honor. He also has valued relationships with other writers and poets who feel the same esteem for the inspiring literary figure.

Literary Works

<u>Books</u>

From Realism to Surrealism

<u>Anthologies</u>

The Muntu Poets of Cleveland Volume 1
Cuyahoga County Library Anthologies Volumes 1 - 4
The Muntu Poets 47 Years Later with Russell Atkins

FROM
REALISM
TO SURREALISM
A BOOK OF POETIC PROSE
BY
YASEEN
ASSAMI
THE BROWN PAPER BAG BLUES...

Gorilla Glue DUCT Tape and Spit

Slipping through the cracks,
fate and tyme call on some patient moment before the
fifth minute.
looking for some sign of success,clinging to a mustard
seed of faith.
Listening to the whispers of deferred dreams,
Dancing on a razors edge,
Looking back at a situation as it clings to the tears of a
soul lost in the confusion of a
frustrated affair.
Watching the bitter chill of winter , caress the promise
of a warm spring day.
Peering through the heat of summer into a glass of
frozen needs of why not.
Dancing with tyme , Looking for your embrace between
the flickering lite of the window
pane and the gentle clatter of a broken lantern that
reflects the frosty patterns of a cat's
meow.
Holding hands with a forgotten commitment,
ages snatches away the care free uncearinty of youth,
Death stands ever so near uttering the names of past
hello's.
Latin rhythms of a flamingo dream reach for the true
colors of tomorrows sweat
drenched efforts of slip and tac.
Slowly moving toward the out stretched arms of
loneliness,

the voices of despair speak about the gentle ways of
truth.
my heart holds the promise of romance,as the gentle
breeze of spring,
hums a love you now as never before.

Sometymes Mother Sings the Blues

LOOKING out my window into the coolness of the sunshi
ne
Realizing the sounds i hear from across the street
Belong to the leaves as they turn from green to gold
to various hues of the blues
Seasons dancing in the wind and me watching birds
sing songs of tomorrow's melodies
Yesterday's ambitions move past in a raging fury
The feeling of fear rushes and roars through my every ef
fort like a steam locamotive
Looking into the eyes of a polymer person realizing
his plastic tung pushes synthetic words
Past the deaf ears of dead men.
Mother sings the blues ,as daddy dances beneath
willow trees
stretching small nothings into
Large provisions.
Watching words from the past turn into peppermint
truths and rubber reasons between me and Dee.
I meet you somewhere in the darker corners of my
mind while reaching for the volume to turn up
The song my mother sang to me in my crib......

THE BROWN PAPER BAG BLUES.

Russell Atkins with members of the Writers Workshop (John Donoghue, Bob Donoghue, John Stickneyam, and Faheem Khabeer (sitting far left)); and some members of the Original Muntu Poets including: Norman Jordan (standing 2nd from left), C.E. Shy (standing 4th from left), Yaseen A. Assami (standing last from left), and Yahya Abdussabur (sitting last from left)
(Photo credit: Diane Kendig)

Tragic Freewill
and Power BLUESTUNEUP

Crawling through popcorn boxes of freewill and madness
only to come from beneath a
book of ethics covered with sounds of death and buckets
of ink.
Words leap over paper spelling out the reasons for
Negros an echoes , counting the
explosions of reality , naming the misery that creeps into
empty spaces of pain and
passion that surround the murders of blind children and
cripple candy.
Calling , speaking ,singing ,saying ,washing away the
cartons of sickness that strike
fear into the hearts and minds of the free choosing will
having desire that circles death
with the call of timeless passion for the poison ways of
sleepless madness.
Choose the way the will takes , time bounds the meaning
of freedom with the laws , as
laughter slings plates of wonder into the faces of hungry
child people , plastic illusions
of fear escape through a key hole into plains of morals
and conduct.
Cause and effect . Is we free , or is we bound by a purple
sounding bowl of necessity ,
ways ,days, nays ,prays timely visions of ancestral
tradition cling heavily to the

foundation of the spirit.
Is the will free? IS the will free? Is the choice the will and
freedom and illusion of
choices thrown to the many by the few who carry the
virus of power to the extreme of
oppression ?
Cries of murder reach the ears of the murderer only to
be justified by the judge and the
blindness of the court , law and order and money and
politics and slavery and freedom
and vice and English and insanity sometimes tells hungry
mothers to kill the choice of
how to choose the way death shall come.
Life leaves us old and helpless shivering at the edge of
the grave watching the choices
we made fade into history.

Yahya Abdussabur

Biographical Information

Yahya Abdussabur/nee (Jon Hall) was born August 11, 1943 in Cleveland Ohio. In 1967, after reading the autobiography of Malcolm X and the Black Nationalist movement, he sought to express this awareness. He was invited to attend a writers' workshop at the opportunities industrialization center, which was located on intersection of Superior Avenue and Ansel Road.

On attending, he was impressed by the black men there and their ability to express themselves by spoken word. He was so impressed that he went home and composed a few poems. This resulted in his being a part of the workshop effort which took the name the Muntu Poets. His membership in the group led to his exposure to a bigger world and to his becoming a devout devotee of Islam that is practiced all over the world.

Literary Works

Anthologies

The Muntu Poets of Cleveland Volume 1
New Black Poetry
The Muntu Poets 47 Years Later with Russell Atkins

Yahya Abdussabur is a contributing writer in the *New Black Poetry* anthology

Change

mind was not made to dwell
on one thought
but to explore and find out
what life is about
people in a rut soon find themselves
enslaved, chained not by iron
  just day to day---Struggle
to free your mind
go and seek fulfillment
find out the beauty that living can bring
understand your fellow man
grasp a thought and follow your star

when i finally realized that
man's struggle would not always
preoccupy me, when i recognized
that there would come the day
when something else would inspire me;
i became confused and dumbfounded
at this aspect of life, but i lay
wait for this grand day-
for the shelf that i'm on leads towards
decay
i would like to speak of that change
i see, a greater meaning for being

Original Muntu Poets (left the right) Yahya Abdussabur,
Mr. Gentleman aka C.E. Shy, and Yaseen Assami.
(Photo Credit: K Kelly McElroy)

Elmer Buford

Biographical Information

Elmer Buford, an original Muntu Poet, was born in Cleveland, Ohio on May 2, 1933. He served in the U.S. Army in Korea and Japan. After his honorable discharge in December, 1955, he took courses at Cuyahoga Community College and Cleveland State University, where he eventually received associate and bachelor degrees respectively.

He authored and published a book named *Conclusions* in 1971 under the pen name B. Felton. Russell Atkins himself wrote the forward for this book. Gaining widespread literary recognition, Buford has been published in the *Broadside Press* (Detroit, Michigan), the *Free Lance*, the *Muntu Journal*, the *Sattvas Review*, the *Vindicator, the Cleveland Record*, and other publications.

Literary Works

<u>Books</u>

Conclusions

<u>Anthologies</u>

The Muntu Poets of Cleveland Volume 1
The Muntu Poets 47 Years Later with Russell Atkins

<u>Publications</u>

The Broadside Press
The Free Lance
The Muntu Journal
The Sattvas Review
The Cleveland Record

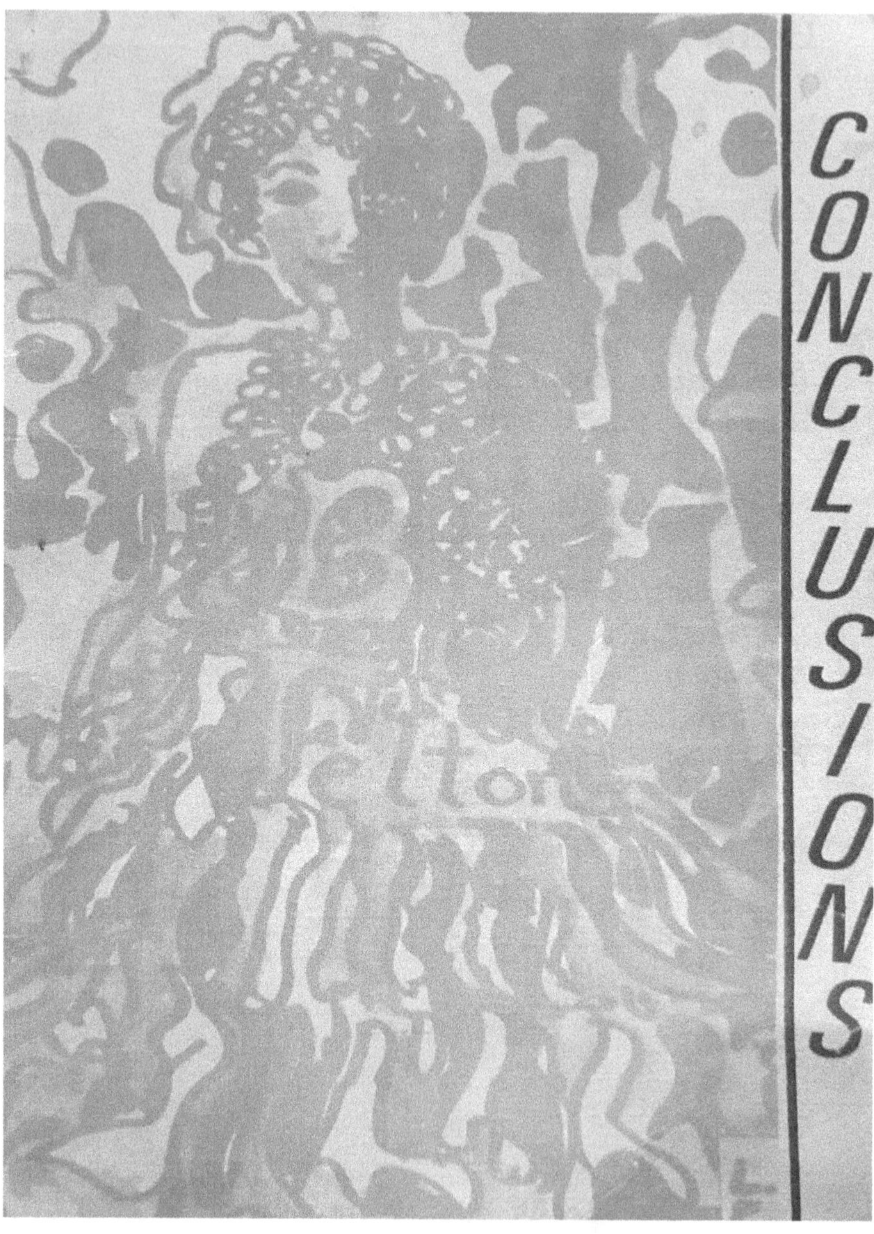

Published 1971, authored by B Felton (aka Elmer Buford), forward by Russell Atkins

Requiem for Strange Bedfellows

The West –South – North-East/
               Winds collide and Ideologies
challenge
Clashing mixed with the wind/
               Corrupted by the blind
ambition of men
That sought to bring political philosophies/
               That ended in abrupt,
swift, agonizing death
Now the gargoyles – the banshi/
               Demons wail terrifying
The subconscious will/
               Visions & nightmares
Of a hideous & obscene/
               Time-place & day
That has etched-immortality/
               The decadence so
Firmly cemented in a/
               Substance called memory
Conflict has no reverence/
               For the silver chalice
As death never leaves/
               Never goes away
A lawless assassin/
               Totally indifferent towards its
Opposition-forever demanding/
               More & more human
sacrifice-

& humanity-executing in/
>The name of peace-brotherhood

& liberty-thus in mud/
>Filled holes of teeming turpitude

Heat the stench of death/
>Putrid flesh rotting as

Mosquitoes-flies-maggots abound/
>As scavengers of

Justice.... Killed, For what? Some-no many/
>Under twenty-killed

Murdered not for what/
>They did-but because of war

In war-at war-into conflict/
>Many slept in the same bed

Trenches or foxholes/
>Side by side-ate from the same

Table or drank from/
>The same cup

And yet America slept/
>Its nocturnal beleaguered

Homo-sapiens swept of de blessing/
>Claire De Leese

The forgotten homo-sapiens/
>Returned home to

The soil of their majesty/
>As strangers in

Abstentia-no roar of/
>Nor from the crowd

Nor the blare of the trumpet/
>Nor the fluttering

Of ticker tape for/

Its unwelcomed sons

hat were truly
Breaking – wrecking fragile alliances/

On warped parchments/
    An invective were
Hustle back & forth/
    In ferocious – corrupt
Manner by near/
    Sighted generals & diplomats
That sought not/
    Abrupt agonizing death

K Kelly with master poet, writer, playwright, composer
and founder of the Muntu Poets, Russell Atkins.
(Photo Credit: C.E. Shy)

THE UNSUNG MASTERS SERIES
RUSSELL ATKINS
On the Life & Work of an American Master
Edited by Kevin Prufer & Michael Dumanis

Russell Atkins reviews recent poetry By Muntu Poet
C.E. Shy
(Photo credit: C.E. Shy 2015)

Norman Jordan was an internationally known poet who made his home in Fayette County, West Virginia. Jordan, pictured here in the African American Heritage Family Tree Museum which he founded in Ansted, West Virginia, was also well-known for his portrayal of figures such as Carter G. Woodson and as a playwright and arts administrator.

Norman Jordan was a member of the Griot Collective
Poetry Workshop of Jackson, Tennessee. In 2008, he
became an official member of the Affrilachian Poets of
Lexington, Kentucky.

Ain't No Change!

Compilation Volume 2, Album Companion Book

UPTOWN

MEDIA JOINT VENTURES
PUBLISHING

UPTOWN

MEDIA JOINT VENTURES
RECORDS